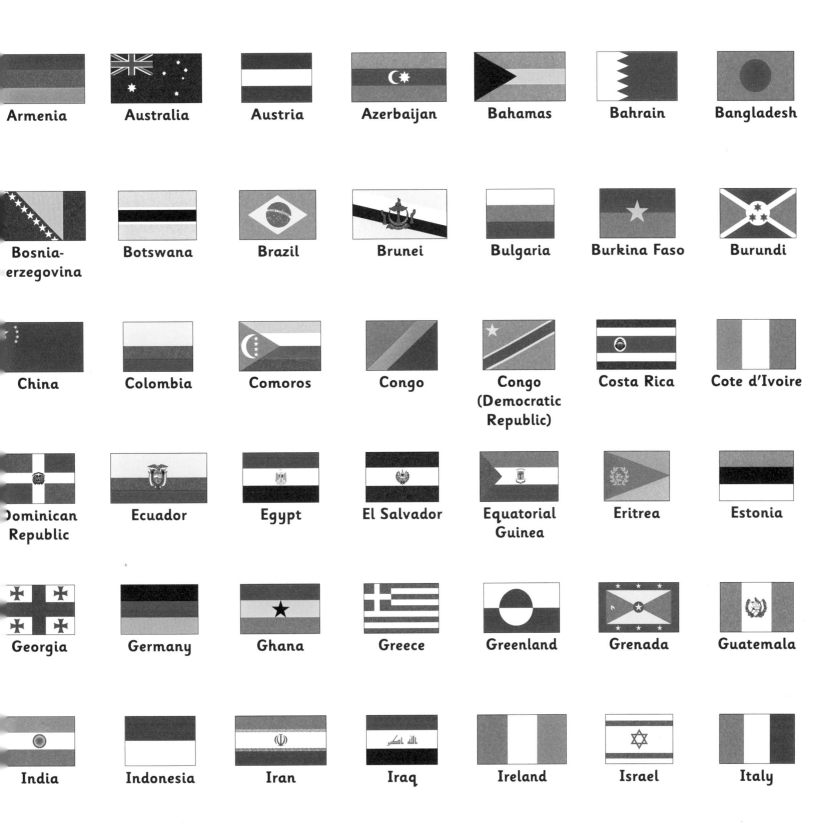

| Armenia | Australia | Austria | Azerbaijan | Bahamas | Bahrain | Bangladesh |

| Bosnia-Herzegovina | Botswana | Brazil | Brunei | Bulgaria | Burkina Faso | Burundi |

| China | Colombia | Comoros | Congo | Congo (Democratic Republic) | Costa Rica | Cote d'Ivoire |

| Dominican Republic | Ecuador | Egypt | El Salvador | Equatorial Guinea | Eritrea | Estonia |

| Georgia | Germany | Ghana | Greece | Greenland | Grenada | Guatemala |

| India | Indonesia | Iran | Iraq | Ireland | Israel | Italy |

| orea, South | Kosovo | Kuwait | Kyrgyzstan | Laos | Latvia | Lebanon |

PHILIP'S

Infant School
Atlas

DAVID WRIGHT AND RACHEL NOONAN

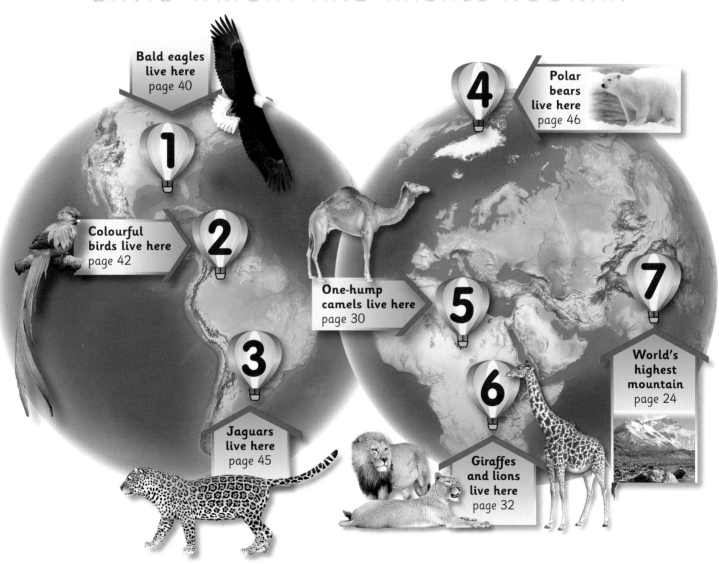

Bald eagles live here page 40

1

Polar bears live here page 46

4

Colourful birds live here page 42

2

One-hump camels live here page 30

5

7

3

World's highest mountain page 24

Jaguars live here page 45

6

Giraffes and lions live here page 32

IN ASSOCIATION WITH
THE ROYAL GEOGRAPHICAL SOCIETY
WITH THE INSTITUTE OF BRITISH GEOGRAPHERS

Royal Geographical Society
with IBG

Advancing geography
and geographical learning

About this Atlas

Message to Adults

Children love discovering new things . . . this atlas has hundreds of new things to discover! Some will even be a surprise for adults!

This is an atlas for young children to enjoy. We can't tell children everything about everywhere, but we *can* take them to some amazing places.

They will find out a lot about the geography, people, climate, plants and animals – as well as some of the problems – of our amazing world!

Don't worry about detailed understanding just yet. The numbered balloons on the maps allow the children to find the places on each map. Every numbered balloon has a corresponding picture and text about that particular *real* place.

As well as beautiful photographs and illustrations, we have included lots of wonderful postage stamps: real messages from real places! There are messages on the flags we have chosen too.

Message to Children

Welcome to this world atlas – let's explore the world together! Our **balloon** takes you to **real places**. You can find where these places are on the **maps**. The **pictures** and **words** tell you more about each place. The authors, **David Wright** and **Rachel Noonan**, love travelling and want you to enjoy our world as much as they do.

You will soon discover things about the world that most grown-ups don't know!

First published in Great Britain in 2009 by Philip's, a division of Octopus Publishing Group Limited (www.octopusbooks.co.uk)
Carmelite House, 50 Victoria Embankment, London EC4Y 0DZ
An Hachette UK Company (www.hachette.co.uk)

To Florence, Molly and Isaac
Text © 2009 David Wright and Rachel Noonan
Maps © 2021 Philip's
First published 2009.
Fourth edition 2021.

Cartography by Philip's

A CIP catalogue record for this book is available from the British Library.

ISBN 978-1-84907-584-8

David Wright and Rachel Noonan have asserted their moral rights under the Copyright, Designs and Patents Act, 1988, to be identified as the authors of this work.

Printed in Italy

Details of other Philip's titles and services can be found on our website at:
www.philips-maps.co.uk

Contents

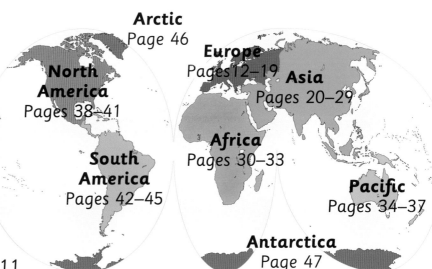

Arctic
Page 46

Europe
Pages 12–19

North America
Pages 38–41

Asia
Pages 20–29

South America
Pages 42–45

Africa
Pages 30–33

Pacific
Pages 34–37

Antarctica
Page 47

Philip's and the Royal Geographical Society

This Philip's atlas displays the logo of the **Royal Geographical Society** (with the **Institute of British Geographers**). The Royal Geographical Society supports education, teaching, research and expeditions. The role of 'promoting public understanding of geography' now reaches 5 to 7 year olds through this new atlas.

Philip's has been publishing good maps for over 150 years.

Find out more about the Royal Geographical Society! Visit their website at www.rgs.org – David Wright is a Fellow and a Chartered Geographer of the RGS.

Royal Geographical Society
with IBG

Advancing geography
and geographical learning

Our Planet in Space

Space is huge! This picture shows the **planets** in our **Solar System**. These planets go round our Sun. But if you look at the sky at night you can see hundreds of **stars**. The stars you see are mostly other suns far, far away.

Sun   Mercury   Venus   Earth   Mars   Jupiter   Saturn   Uranus   Neptune

How long does it take for the planets to go round the Sun? They are all different. **Earth** takes **365 days** (1 year). **Mercury** only takes **88 Earth-days**, but **Neptune** takes **165 Earth-years** to circle the Sun!

Did you know?
The planets of the Solar System are very different sizes, and the Sun is huge! If the **Sun** was the size of a basketball then **Jupiter** (the biggest planet) would be the size of a pea, and the **Earth** would be smaller than a full stop!

8 planets circle the Sun. How can you remember the planets? Here is a funny sentence to help you. Can you think of an even funnier sentence to help you remember the order of the planets, using the first letter of each planet?

Mercury	My	M..........
Venus	Very	V...........
Earth	Excellent	E...........
Mars	Mother	M..........
Jupiter	Just	J...........
Saturn	Served	S...........
Uranus	Us	U.........
Neptune	Noodles	N..........

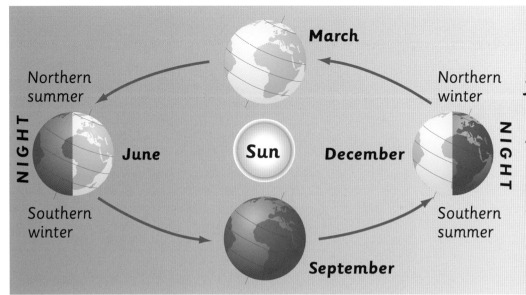

March

Northern summer

June

NIGHT

Southern winter

Sun

September

Northern winter

December

NIGHT

Southern summer

Winter is when our part of the Earth is **tilted away from the Sun**, and gets **less sunlight** and **heat**. **Summer** is when our part of the Earth is **tilted to get more sunlight** and **heat**. Tropical lands get the most heat from the Sun; Arctic lands get the least heat.

Can you be the Earth going round the Sun?
Use a ball. Spin it all the way round. This is one day. Now get a friend to stand still – they can be the Sun. Walk all the way round your friend spinning the world **365 times**!
This is one year!

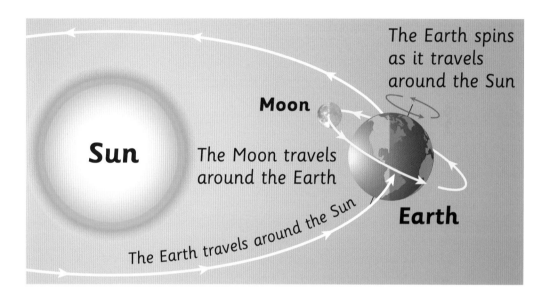

Sun

Moon

The Moon travels around the Earth

Earth

The Earth spins as it travels around the Sun

The Earth travels around the Sun

Our planet is so beautiful!
Can you find where **YOU** live? Find the names of the continents on pages 10–11.

What makes Earth such a GOOD planet to live on?
The **Sun** makes us warm. We've got **land** to live on. We've got **soil** for crops. We've got **air** to breathe. We've got **water** to drink. We've got **coal**, **oil**, **sun** and **wind** for energy. We've got **friends** too! Can you think of more good reasons to live here?

Our Planet Earth is ...

1 ... so beautiful!

Imagine you are in a spacecraft; you look out of the window and see **THIS!**

Wow! You can see blue **oceans**, white **clouds** and green **land**.

2 ... so varied

Our artist has put 4 amazing places on 1 picture!
Can you find...
... cold, icy Antarctica (find out more on page **47**),
... hot, sandy desert (see page **30**),
... tall fir forest by a lake (see page **20**),
... a city with skyscrapers (see page **29**)?

CAN YOU FIND...
North America? (Find out more on page **38**.)
South America? (See page **44**.)
Some islands? (See page **43**.)

3 ... a sphere

An easy shape to understand. If you've caught a ball, you know the shape of our planet! (See page **4**.)

4 ... so light – and so dark!

In one whole year every place on Earth has **equal time in light and darkness** – half and half. [**It's true!**]

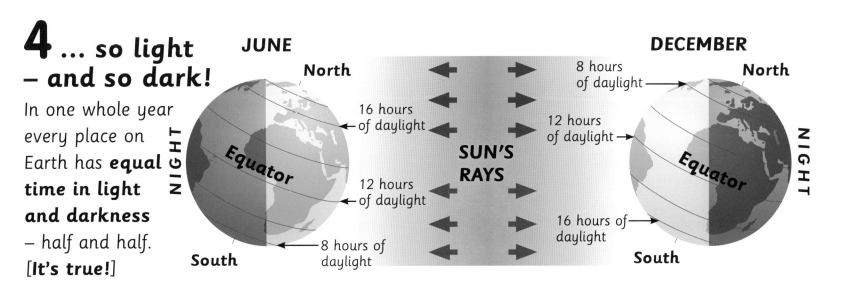

JUNE

North

NIGHT

Equator

South

16 hours of daylight

12 hours of daylight

8 hours of daylight

SUN'S RAYS

DECEMBER

8 hours of daylight

12 hours of daylight

16 hours of daylight

North

NIGHT

Equator

South

It is so easy to work out the shortest routes for aeroplanes!

To find the shortest route by air on a globe:

1 Find your start point (**A**).

2 Find your end point (**B**).

3 Put a piece of string between your start point and end point.

4 Pull the string tight – and that's the shortest route!

Surprise! From **London** (**A**) to **Los Angeles** (**B**), the shortest route goes over **Greenland**!

A

B

ATLANTIC OCEAN

But it is so difficult to put the world on a flat map!

Find out more on page **8**. This stamp from **Canada** shows one way of keeping shapes right – do you like it?

COMMONWEALTH DAY
JOUR DU COMMONWEALTH
1983/03/14

$2 CANADA

But – we pollute our planet in lots of ways.

We put rubbish on the **land** and in the **sea**.
We pollute the **air**.

We spoil our **soils**.
We cut down **trees**.
We catch too many **fish**.

Understanding Maps

The best way to understand maps is to **USE maps!**

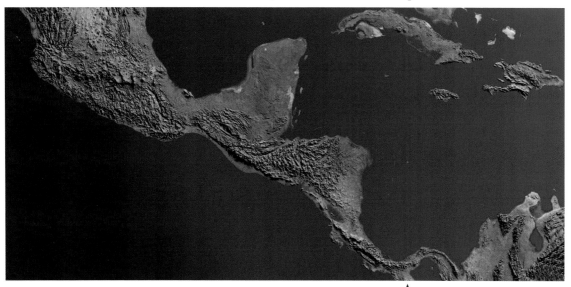

This is a **SATELLITE IMAGE** of Central America. ↑

This is a **MAP** of Central America. ↑

Here is an image taken from a satellite in space. Look at the image and the map. Can you find: the **land**, the **sea**, **islands**, a **lake**, and some **mountains**?

Here is a map of the same places. **Can you spot some differences?** A map is like a picture taken from the air. A map can tell you a lot more than a picture: the names of cities, rivers and mountains, and borders where countries begin and end.

The satellite image does not show any borders.
Can you see which **map colour** is used for the **sea** and the **rivers**?*
Can you see which **map colour** is used for **borders**?*

Maps can be of very big places, or of small places.
Can you draw a map of your bedroom? A globe is a map of the whole world. Maps are usually flat, but a **globe** is a map and it is a **sphere**!

*Find answers on page 9

What can maps tell us?

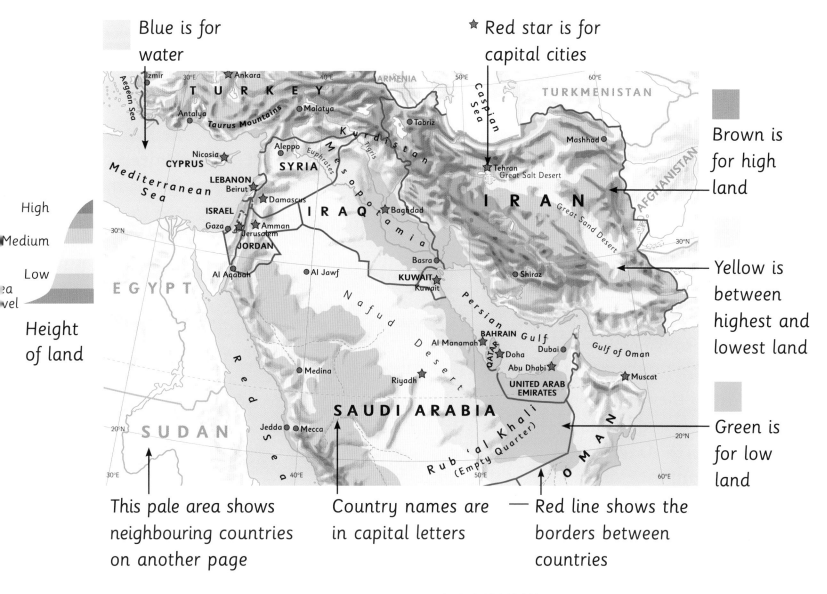

Blue is for water

Red star is for capital cities

Brown is for high land

Yellow is between highest and lowest land

Green is for low land

High
Medium
Low
Sea level

Height of land

This pale area shows neighbouring countries on another page

Country names are in capital letters

Red line shows the borders between countries

This is the scale bar. It tells you how far **1 centimetre** on the map is on the real world!

Scale 1:22,000,000   1 cm on the map = 220 km on the ground
0   220 km   500 km   1,000 km   1,500 km   2,000 km

0   1   2   3   4   cm   5   6   7   8   9

Where in the world?

This little map of the world is on every page. It shows you where in the world the big map is. It also shows you how big that bit of the world is.

Use a globe as well! Only globes always have the right size and the right shape for all parts of the world.

Map makers

(cartographers) are so careful to make maps accurate that you can even use a map to find out how far it is from one place to another place.

Oceans, Continents and Countries

United Nations.
This is the flag of the United Nations.

This map shows our whole world.

Our 7 continents are named in big, bold letters like this: **EUROPE**. Our world has **5 oceans** – can you name them? A..., A..., I..., P..., and S....

The **'Top 10' countries** are named on this map. These countries have the most people. Find the **blue** people with **white** numbers. China has the most people, so is number 1. India is 2, USA is 3 and so on. Most of the 'Top 10' are in Asia, but can you find ...

ONE in **North America**?*
[This is easy!]

ONE in **South America**?*

ONE in **Africa**?*

'TOP 10' COUNTRIES:

1. **China** 1,398 million people
2. **India** 1,339 million people
3. **USA** 335 million people
4. **Indonesia** 275 million people
5. **Pakistan** 238 million people
6. **Nigeria** 220 million people
7. **Brazil** 213 million people
8. **Bangladesh** 164 million people
9. **Russia** 142 million people
10. **Mexico** 130 million people

The **Atlantic Ocean** is **7 times bigger** than the **Arctic Ocean**.

The **Pacific Ocean** is **HUGE! GIGANTIC! ENORMOUS!** It is bigger than **ALL** the world's land!

CANADA

NORTH AMERICA

USA

MEXICO

ATLANTIC OCEAN

PACIFIC OCEAN

BRAZIL

SOUTH AMERICA

ANTARCTICA

Arctic Circle

Tropic of Cancer

Equator

Tropic of Capricorn

Antarctic Circle

*Find answers on page 48

The 'BIG 6' countries. ① ② ③ ④ ⑤ ⑥ **There are 6 very big countries** – our map shows them all. We can all see the biggest country: **Russia**! It is over 17 million square kilometres in area.

'BIG 6': a list of all the countries with more than 4 million square kilometres of land.

① **Russia** Over 17 million
② **Canada** Nearly 10 million
③ **USA** Over 9 million
④ **China** Over 9 million
⑤ **Brazil** Over 8 million
⑥ **Australia** Over 7 million

The 'snip' at the bottom of the map allows continents to be the right **SIZE** and the right **SHAPE**. Many world maps make the cold lands too **BIG** and the hot lands too **SMALL**. Our map gets it right!

A stamp from Fiji. The Pacific Ocean is in the middle!

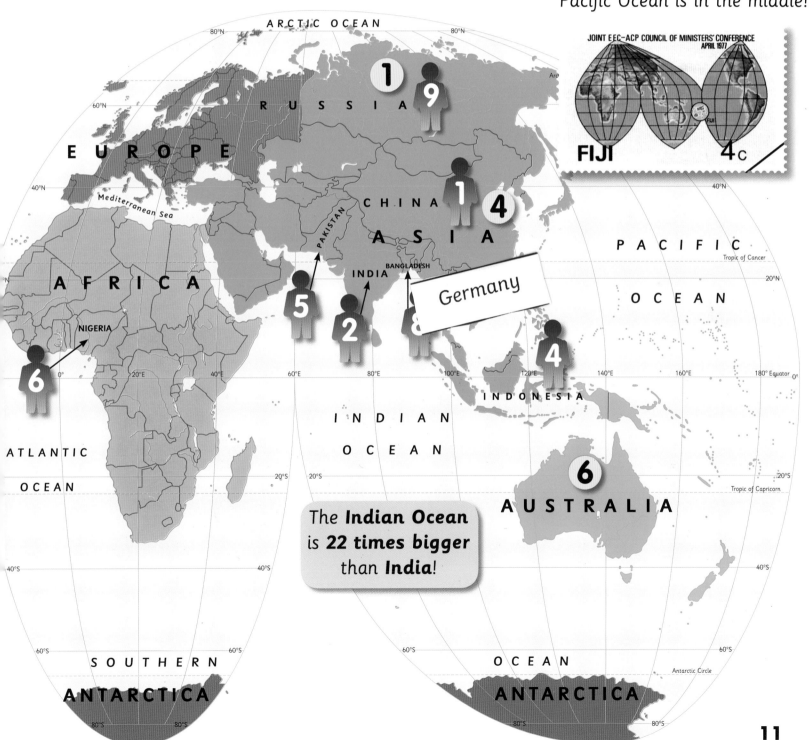

The **Indian Ocean is 22 times bigger** than **India**!

Germany

Discover...
the British Isles

1 Can you see the houses of Parliament and Big Ben? This is where the government of the United Kingdom meets to make new laws.

This giant wheel takes you up, so that you can see London from the air.

2 These amazing stones were put up without diggers or cranes. This is **Stonehenge**; it was built by the people who lived in Britain about 4,000 years ago!

3 This is a little train for big people! Now it carries tourists, but it used to carry slate. **100 years ago** there was a lot of mining in **Wales**. Welsh slate makes really good roofs.

4 This bridge is so amazing! This picture is on a £1 coin! It was built for trains by the Victorians over 100 years ago. The **Forth Bridge** was the first big bridge made of steel.

6 This cross is special. It is an old Celtic cross in **Ireland**. Can you draw the pattern carved on it?

5 **Scotland** has big mountains and great wildlife. This is **Ben Nevis**, the highest mountain in the British Isles. **Can you** see what the osprey will have for dinner?

To the North Pole
page 46

This way to Canada page 39

Did you know? The Shetland Islands are much nearer to **NORWAY** than to London! (See map on page 15.)

The Union Jack...

England + Scotland + St Patrick

...is made from **THREE FLAGS**!

7 The flag of Ireland: Green for Catholics; Orange for Protestants; and White in the middle for peace in Ireland.

This way to Western Europe page 15

This way to the Mediterranean page 17

Scale 1:5,500,000   1 cm on the map = 55 km on the ground

| 0 | 55 km | 100 km | 200 km | 300 km | 400 km | 500 km |

0   1   2   3   4   cm 5   6   7   8   9

Map labels

ATLANTIC OCEAN

Shetland Islands
Lerwick

Orkney Islands
Kirkwall

Cape Wrath
Thurso

Lewis
Stornoway
St Kilda
Outer Hebrides

North West Highlands
Inverness
Aviemore
Aberdeen

Portree
Skye
Inner Hebrides

Ben Nevis
Fort William

SCOTLAND
Dundee

Mull
Oban
Stirling
Glasgow
Clyde
Firth of Forth
Edinburgh
Berwick-upon-Tweed

Arran
Southern Uplands

North Sea

Derry/Londonderry
Donegal
NORTHERN IRELAND
Sligo
Belfast

North Channel
Dumfries
Carlisle
Tyne
Newcastle-upon-Tyne

Isle of Man
Douglas

Scarborough

IRELAND
Galway
Dublin

Irish Sea
Anglesey

York
Blackpool
Leeds

Shannon
Limerick

Liverpool
Manchester
Sheffield
Lincoln

UNITED KINGDOM

Wexford
Wrexham
ENGLAND
Nottingham
Norwich

Shrewsbury
Leicester
Birmingham

Killarney
Aberystwyth
WALES
Cambridge
Ipswich

Cork
Brecon
Severn
Gloucester
Oxford
Thames

Carmarthen
Swansea
Cardiff
Bristol
Salisbury
London

Hastings

Exeter
Portsmouth
Isle of Wight
FRANCE

Penzance
Truro
Plymouth
Isles of Scilly
English Channel

Discover...
Western Europe

1 **Over 1,000 years ago the Vikings sailed from Norway.** Viking boats were amazing. People could sail them, row them and even carry them! Vikings sailed to many lands

2 **Reindeer live in the far north.** The far north of Europe is inside the **Arctic Circle**. Find out more on page 46.

3 **Why do people decorate trees at Christmas?** The tradition of Christmas trees came from **Germany**. Now Christians all over the world decorate trees in their homes at Christmas time – the 'birthday' of Jesus.

4 **The European Union has its head office in Belgium. SURPRISE!** The walls are made of ... **GLASS!**

Lego was invented by a toymaker in **Denmark.** Legoland is near the factory where it is made.

5 The Arc de Triomphe is in Paris, the capital of France.

5 The Arc de Triomphe is in Paris, the capital of France. The words mean 'triumphal arch'. It lists the victories of Emperor Napoleon.

6 Skiing is fun in the Alps in winter. The high snowy mountains of **Switzerland** make good ski slopes in winter.

Scale 1:17,500,000   1 cm on the map = 175 km on the ground

0   175 km   500 km   1,000 km   1,500 km

To the North Pole page 46

This way to Russia page 21

This way to USA page 41

To Africa page 31

ICELAND
Reykjavik
Arctic Circle
Norwegian Sea
Faroe Islands
ATLANTIC OCEAN
Shetland Islands
Orkney Islands
Hebrides
Inverness
Aberdeen
Glasgow   Edinburgh
North Sea
DENMARK   Copenhagen
Belfast
IRELAND
Dublin
Limerick
Manchester
UNITED KINGDOM
Cork
Birmingham
Cardiff
London
Plymouth
English Channel
Channel Islands
Bay of Biscay
Bordeaux
FRANCE
Toulouse
Pyrenees
PORTUGAL
SPAIN
Seine
Paris
Strasbourg
Luxembourg
LUXEMBOURG
Brussels
BELGIUM
Bonn
NETHERLANDS
Amsterdam
Hamburg
Berlin
GERMANY
Frankfurt
Rhine
Munich
Salzburg
Berne
SWITZERLAND
Geneva
LIECHTENSTEIN
Vienna
AUSTRIA
Danube
Rhone
Avignon
Nice
Marseilles
Corsica
ITALY
Adriatic Sea
Tyrrhenian Sea
Mediterranean Sea
Ionian Sea
GREECE
MALTA
TUNISIA
MOROCCO
ALGERIA
NORWAY
SWEDEN
Lapland
Tromso
Trondheim
Bergen
Oslo
Stockholm
Kokkola
FINLAND
Helsinki
Barents Sea
RUSSIA
ESTONIA
LATVIA
LITHUANIA
BELARUS
POLAND
UKRAINE
CZECHIA
SLOVAKIA
HUNGARY
SLOVENIA
CROATIA
ROMANIA
BOSNIA-HERZEGOVINA
SERBIA
KOSOVO
MONTENEGRO
NORTH MACEDONIA
ALBANIA
Baltic Sea

Discover...
Mediterranean
Europe

1 A procession to remember Jesus in Burgos.
The days before Easter in **Spain** are called **Semana Santa** (Holy Week). There are processions every day. People feel sad but on Easter Day everyone feels happy again.

2 **This is the flag of Slovenia:** the shield shows the three peaks of Mount Triglav.

3 **The Colosseum in Rome.** Lots of buildings in **Rome** were built by the Romans over **2,000 years ago**. Now millions of people live here, so there are lots of new buildings and cars too.

4 **This is a new bridge that looks old.** The old bridge was blown up in the war in **Bosnia** in 1993. Now there is peace – and the bridge has been built again, just like the old bridge.

5 **This temple is over 2,000 years old.** It is called the **Parthenon**. It is in **Athens**, the capital city of Greece. How many columns can you count? Do you know any words that come from Greek words? Clue: find words with 'ph': they come from Greece!

6 **What is growing here?** These are **olive trees** in Crete. Olives and grapes grow well in Mediterranean lands. Why? Remember the 5 Ws: '**Warm Wet Westerly Winds** in **Winter**'.

7 **There are lots of fish in the Mediterranean Sea.** Fish is good food and tourists like to eat fish. But there are two problems: over-fishing and pollution. This photo shows a fish shop in **Naples**, **Italy**.

Scale 1:15,000,000   1 cm on the map = 150 km on the ground

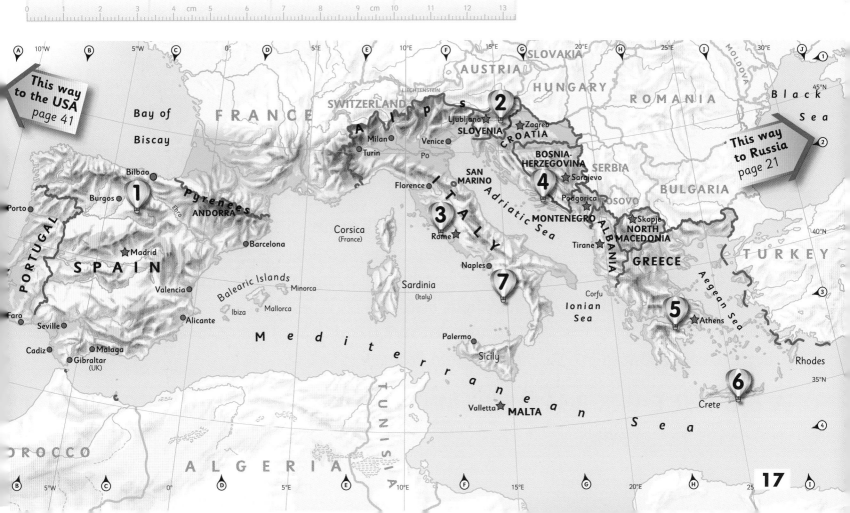

This way to the USA page 41

This way to Russia page 21

Discover...
Eastern Europe

1 **This market is in Krakow,** a city in the south of **Poland.** Tourists come to see the beautiful buildings. Do you have local shops selling Polish food? Can you find **pierogi** (dumplings) or **golabki** (cabbage rolls)?

2 **Which ALPHABET or АЛФАВИТ?**
Belarus and Ukraine use the Russian Cyrillic alphabet. Try writing your name using the key below!

3 **Children in Ukraine** are folk-dancing. It's fun – and a good way to find out about history.
Did you know? Ukraine is bigger than France!

4 **Skiers catch this train.** They travel through snowy forests to the Carpathian Mountains in **Slovakia**.

А	Б	В	Г	Д	Е	Ё	Ж	З	И	Й	К	Л	М	Н	О	П	Р	С	Т	У	Ф	Х	Ц	Ч	Ш	Щ	Ю	Я
A	B	V	G	D	E	YO	ZH	Z	I	Y	K	L	M	N	O	P	R	S	T	U	F	KH	TS	CH	SH	SHCH	YU	YA

1987

SWEDEN
DENMARK
WEST EAST
GERMANY
POLAND
CZECHOSLOVAKIA
AUSTRIA
HUNGARY
ROMANIA
YUGOSLAVIA
SAN MARINO
ITALY
ALBANIA
BULGARIA
UNION OF SOVIET SOCIALIST REPUBLICS
Baltic Sea
Adriatic Sea
Black Sea

Today

ESTONIA
SWEDEN
DENMARK
LATVIA
LITHUANIA
(RUSSIA)
RUSSIA
BELARUS
GERMANY
POLAND
CZECHIA
SLOVAKIA
UKRAINE
AUSTRIA
HUNGARY
MOLDOVA
SLOVENIA
CROATIA
ROMANIA
SAN MARINO
ITALY
BOSNIA-HERZEGOVINA
SERBIA
MONTENEGRO
KOSOVO
BULGARIA
ALBANIA
NORTH MACEDONIA
Baltic Sea
Adriatic Sea
Black Sea

Spot the differences!

Lots of the countries of Eastern Europe were not on the map in 1987. Can you find some?
Spot **6** new countries*
– **well done!**
Spot **8** – **excellent!**
Spot **10** – **FANTASTIC!**

5 **The River Danube passes through 8 countries.**
It flows from Germany to the Black Sea. This boat **pushes** big barges.

Scale 1:16,000,000 1 cm on the map = 160 km on the ground

| 0 | 160 km | 500 km | 1,000 km | 1,500 km | 2,000 km |

0 1 2 3 4 cm 5 6 7 8 9 cm 10 11 12

This way to the Arctic
page 46

Can you find 2 big seas beginning with B?*

This way to Russia
page 21

To Africa
page 31

NORWAY
SWEDEN
FINLAND
Tallinn
ESTONIA
Baltic Sea
DENMARK
Riga
LATVIA
LITHUANIA
Gdansk
(RUSSIA)
Vilnius
Minsk
GERMANY
BELARUS
RUSSIA
POLAND
Warsaw
CZECHIA
Prague
Krakow
Kiev
Kharkiv
SLOVAKIA
Lvov
Dneister
AUSTRIA
Danube
Bratislava
Carpathian Mountains
UKRAINE
Lugansk
Budapest
HUNGARY
Lake Balaton
MOLDOVA
Donetsk
Ljubljana
SLOVENIA
Zagreb
Subotica
Chisinau
CROATIA
ROMANIA
Odessa
Sea of Azov
BOSNIA-HERZEGOVINA
Belgrade
Brasov
Transylvanian Alps
RUSSIA
SERBIA
Bucharest
Sevastopol
(under Russian control)
Sarajevo
Danube
Constanta
MONTENEGRO
Podgorica
Balkan Mountains
Black Sea
Pristina
KOSOVO
Sofia
BULGARIA
GEORGIA
ITALY
ALBANIA
Skopje
NORTH MACEDONIA
GREECE
TURKEY

Discover...
Russia and its Neighbours

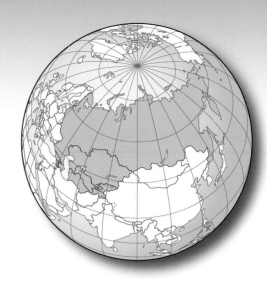

1 **Kamchatka has lots of volcanoes!**
They are part of the Pacific Ring of Fire
– the volcanoes all round the Pacific Ocean.
We are still in **Russia**, but we're nearer
to North America than to Moscow!

2 **Trams are good
for travel in cities.**
Many Russian
cities have trams, with
rails and electric wires.

3 **Lake Baikal is the
deepest lake in the
world.** Winters are so
cold here that they laid
the Trans-Siberian railway
across the frozen lake!
Now the railway goes
round the edge.

**Russian dolls are made
of wood –**
they are **NOT**
cuddly!

4 **The world's
biggest forest!**
The forest of Siberian
Russia is far bigger than
any other forest. This is
a **coniferous forest**:
the trees have cones.
The lake is frozen in
winter.

5 The tundra of Northern Russia is very cold in winter – but reindeer like it! In summer it is marshy because the ground underneath is still frozen. But in some places, there is deep melting in summer.

6 A beautiful mosque in Samarkand, Uzbekistan. Most people in Uzbekistan are Muslims.

7 The Caspian Sea is shared by 5 countries. Can you name some of them?* In wet years the sea grows bigger; in dry years it is smaller. Seals live here. This seal is on the ice.

15 TÜRKMENISTAN
Phoca caspica · Düwlen
1993

Scale 1:40 000 000 1 cm on the map = 400 km on the ground

0	410 km	1,000 km	2,000 km	3,000 km	4,000 km	5,000 km

GREENLAND

Norwegian Sea

Arctic Circle

NORWAY SWEDEN FINLAND ESTONIA LATVIA LITHUANIA BELARUS

ARCTIC OCEAN

Barents Sea

White Sea

Murmansk
Archangel
St Petersburg
Smolensk
Moscow
Nizhniy Novgorod
Yekaterinburg
Saratov
Ufa
Orenburg
Volgograd
Rostov
Astrakhan
Narodnaya
Ural Mountains

This way to the Arctic page 46

Taimyr Peninsula
Norilsk
Yenisei
Ob
Irtysh
Ob
Nizhnevartovsk
Tomsk
Novosibirsk
Omsk
Yenisei

Laptev Sea

East Siberian Sea

Siberia
Lena
Yakutsk
Verkhoyansk Range
Kolyma
Kolyma Range

Bering Strait

Bering Sea

Kamchatka

Sea of Okhotsk
Okhotsk
Sakhalin

Arctic Circle

5

4

3
Krasnoyarsk
Lake Baikal
Irkutsk
Chita
Stanovoy Range
Yablonovyy Range
Amur

Khabarovsk

To the USA page 41

2
Vladivostok

Sea of Japan

To Eastern Europe page 19

Don
Volga
Ural
Caspian Sea
Elbrus
GEORGIA Tbilisi
ARMENIA Yerevan
AZER-BAIJAN Baku
KEY

Nur-Sultan

KAZAKHSTAN

Lake Balkhash

MONGOLIA

NORTH KOREA
SOUTH KOREA
JAPAN

PACIFIC OCEAN

7
Aral Sea
Syrdarya
UZBEKISTAN
Urgench
TURKMENISTAN
Ashgabat
Samarkand
Dushanbe
TAJIKISTAN

6
Almaty
Bishkek
KYRGYZSTAN
Tashkent
Tian Shan
Altai

To India and Southern Asia page 25

CHINA

IRAN

To Middle East page 23

Discover...
the Middle East

The Dome of the Rock is an Islamic monument. Before that there was probably a Christian church and before that a Roman temple and a Jewish temple.

1 **Jerusalem means 'Place of Peace'.** It is a holy city for 3 big religions: Islam, Judaism and Christianity.

Religion	Symbol	Holy day
Islam	☪	Friday
Judaism	✡	Saturday
Christianity	✝	Sunday

2 **Petra in Jordan was once a 'lost city'.** Now the ruins are visited by thousands of people! **Amazing!** This temple was carved out of solid rock!

Did you know?
The Middle East is the only place where **3 continents** meet. Can you name them?* The map on page 23 will help you.

3 **Baghdad is the capital of Iraq.** Can you see the bridge? It goes over the river Euphrates. Can you find it on the map? How many turquoise domes can you see?

4 Muslims all over the world pray facing Mecca. One of the 5 pillars of Islam is to pray 5 times a day; another is to visit Mecca at least once.

5 Much of the Middle East is very dry, so irrigating (watering) the land is very important. This stamp from **Oman** shows an irrigation channel. What else can you see in the picture?*

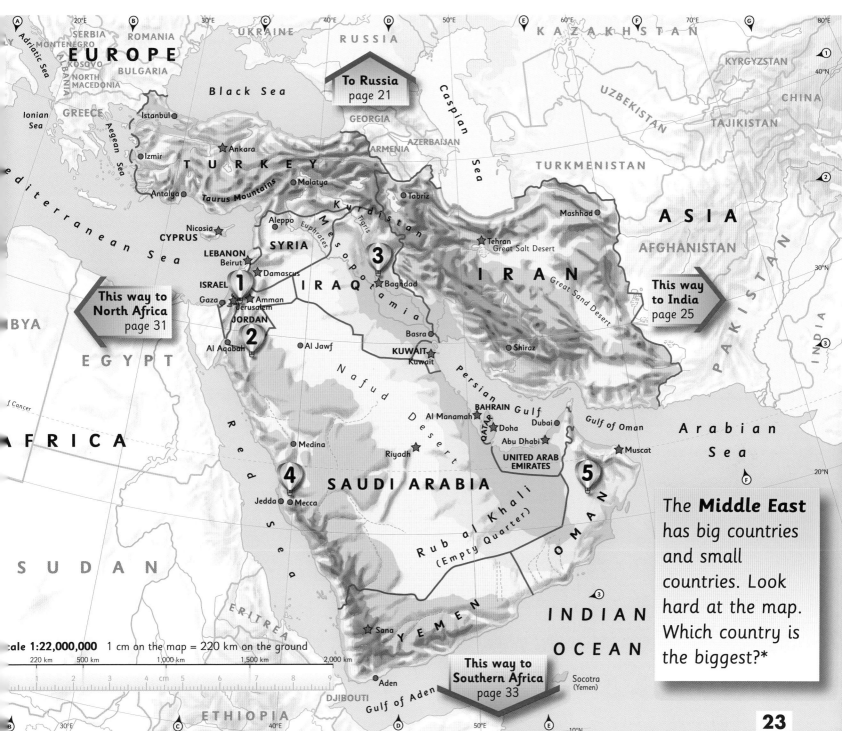

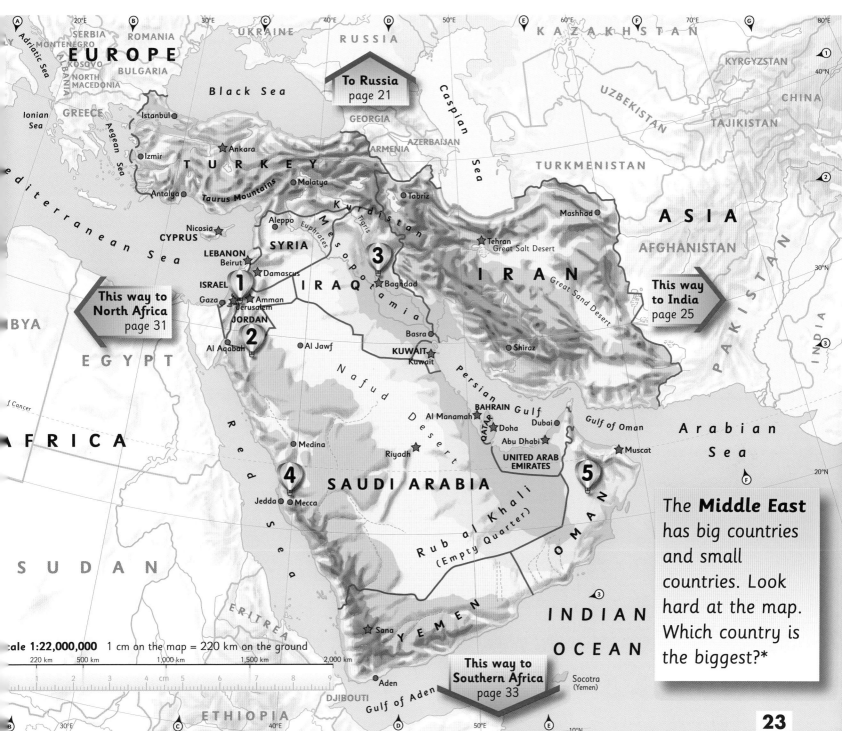

To Russia
page 21

This way to North Africa
page 31

This way to India
page 25

This way to Southern Africa
page 33

The **Middle East** has big countries and small countries. Look hard at the map. Which country is the biggest?*

Scale 1:22,000,000   1 cm on the map = 220 km on the ground

220 km   500 km   1,000 km   1,500 km   2,000 km

EUROPE

SERBIA
MONTENEGRO
KOSOVO
ALBANIA
NORTH MACEDONIA
ROMANIA
BULGARIA
GREECE

Adriatic Sea
Ionian Sea
Aegean Sea
Mediterranean Sea

UKRAINE
RUSSIA
KAZAKHSTAN
KYRGYZSTAN
CHINA
UZBEKISTAN
TAJIKISTAN
ASIA
AFGHANISTAN
PAKISTAN
INDIA

Black Sea
Caspian Sea
GEORGIA
ARMENIA
AZERBAIJAN
TURKMENISTAN

Istanbul
Izmir
Ankara
Antalya
TURKEY
Taurus Mountains
Malatya
Tabriz
Mashhad
Nicosia
CYPRUS
Aleppo
Euphrates
Tigris
Kurdistan
Tehran
Great Salt Desert
LEBANON
Beirut
SYRIA
Mesopotamia
Baghdad
IRAN
Great Sand Desert
ISRAEL
Damascus
Gaza
Jerusalem
Amman
JORDAN
IRAQ
Basra
Shiraz
Al Aqabah
Al Jawf
KUWAIT
Kuwait
Nafud
Persian Gulf
LIBYA
EGYPT
Medina
Riyadh
Red Sea
Desert
Al Manamah
BAHRAIN
QATAR
Doha
Dubai
Abu Dhabi
UNITED ARAB EMIRATES
Gulf
Gulf of Oman
Muscat
Arabian Sea
AFRICA
SUDAN
SAUDI ARABIA
Jedda
Mecca
Rub al Khali (Empty Quarter)
OMAN
ERITREA
YEMEN
Sana
Aden
Socotra (Yemen)
INDIAN OCEAN
DJIBOUTI
Gulf of Aden
ETHIOPIA

23

Discover...
India and Southern Asia

1 **Afghanistan has high mountains, dry deserts and lonely ruins.** But wars have made it a very hard place to live in.

Did you know?
3 religions started in India – **Hinduism**, **Sikhism** and **Buddhism**. Lots of different languages are spoken in India – and many of them have their own alphabet. **Islam** is the main religion in Afghanistan, Pakistan and Bangladesh.

2 **Pakistan is mostly desert**, yet it has more people than any country in Europe or Africa. How can so many people live here? The **River Indus** brings water all year from the high mountains.

4 **Yaks are amazing animals!** People come to the Himalayas to climb the highest moutains in the world. Yaks help to carry all the things the people need. All yaks need is water, grass and their thick fur!

3 **This is the Taj Mahal.** Over 1,000 elephants were used to bring stone to build this beautiful building.

6 In Sri Lanka, tea grows in high mountains – where the days are hot and the nights are cold. Tea-pickers take 2 leaves from each stalk and put them in the baskets on their backs.

5 Mumbai (Bombay) is a big city. Some people here are rich, but many are very poor.

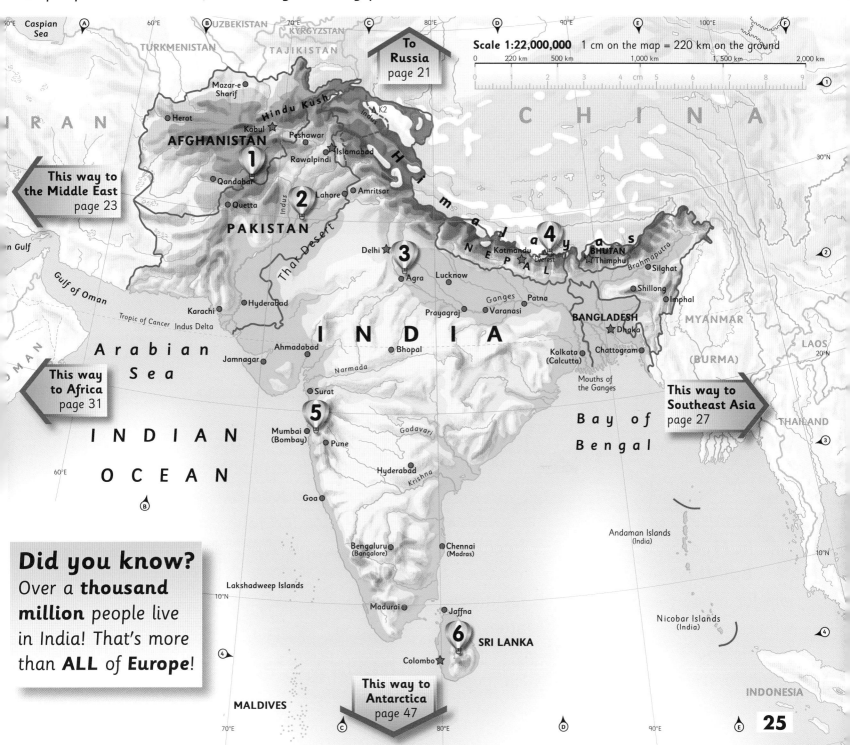

Scale 1:22,000,000   1 cm on the map = 220 km on the ground

To Russia page 21

This way to the Middle East page 23

This way to Africa page 31

This way to Southeast Asia page 27

This way to Antarctica page 47

Did you know? Over a **thousand million** people live in India! That's more than **ALL** of Europe!

Caspian Sea
UZBEKISTAN
KYRGYZSTAN
TURKMENISTAN
TAJIKISTAN
IRAN
Mazar-e Sharif
Herat
Hindu Kush
K2
Kabul
Peshawar
AFGHANISTAN
Rawalpindi
Islamabad
Qandahar
Lahore
Amritsar
Quetta
Indus
PAKISTAN
Thar Desert
n Gulf
Gulf of Oman
Delhi
Agra
Lucknow
NEPAL
Katmandu
Everest
Himalayas
BHUTAN
Thimphu
Brahmaputra
Silghat
Shillong
Imphal
Karachi
Hyderabad
Ganges
Patna
Tropic of Cancer
Indus Delta
Prayagraj
Varanasi
BANGLADESH
Dhaka
MYANMAR
(BURMA)
Arabian Sea
Ahmadabad
Jamnagar
I N D I A
Bhopal
Narmada
Kolkata (Calcutta)
Chattogram
Mouths of the Ganges
Surat
Mumbai (Bombay)
Pune
Godavari
Bay of Bengal
LAOS
THAILAND
Hyderabad
Krishna
I N D I A N
Goa
O C E A N
CHINA
Andaman Islands (India)
Bengaluru (Bangalore)
Chennai (Madras)
Lakshadweep Islands
Madurai
Jaffna
Nicobar Islands (India)
6 SRI LANKA
Colombo
MALDIVES
INDONESIA

Discover...
Southeast Asia

Rice is planted in flooded fields. But water runs down hills! So – how do you grow rice on a slope? Look at Balloon 6 for a clue.

2 **A beautiful palace in Bangkok**, the capital city of Thailand. How many spires can you count?

3 **This is the flag of Cambodia.** In the centre is a drawing of the temple of Angkor Wat.

4 **Fishing in Vietnam** – these round fishing boats are in the South China Sea. Fish is good food, but too much fishing causes too few fish.

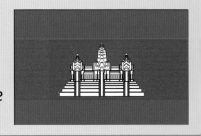

1 **In Myanmar many boys become Buddhist monks.** Sometimes they join for a few weeks, sometimes for their whole lives. They wear special clothes, like the boy in this picture. People respect monks and are happy to give them food.

5 Where does rubber come from?

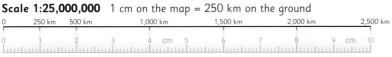
GETAH
Hevea
brasiliensis
WILAYAH PERSEKUTUAN
Malaysia 15¢

This is a rubber tree in a plantation in **Malaysia**. The rubber is the sap of the tree. Some can be 'tapped' and collected.

6 Can you see where people have cut steps into the hill?

These are flat places (called terraces) to plant rice and hold the water. This means that lots of rice can be grown even on steep slopes.

Scale 1:25,000,000   1 cm on the map = 250 km on the ground

0	250 km	500 km	1,000 km	1,500 km	2,000 km	2,500 km

0 1 2 3 cm 4 5 6 7 8 9 cm 10

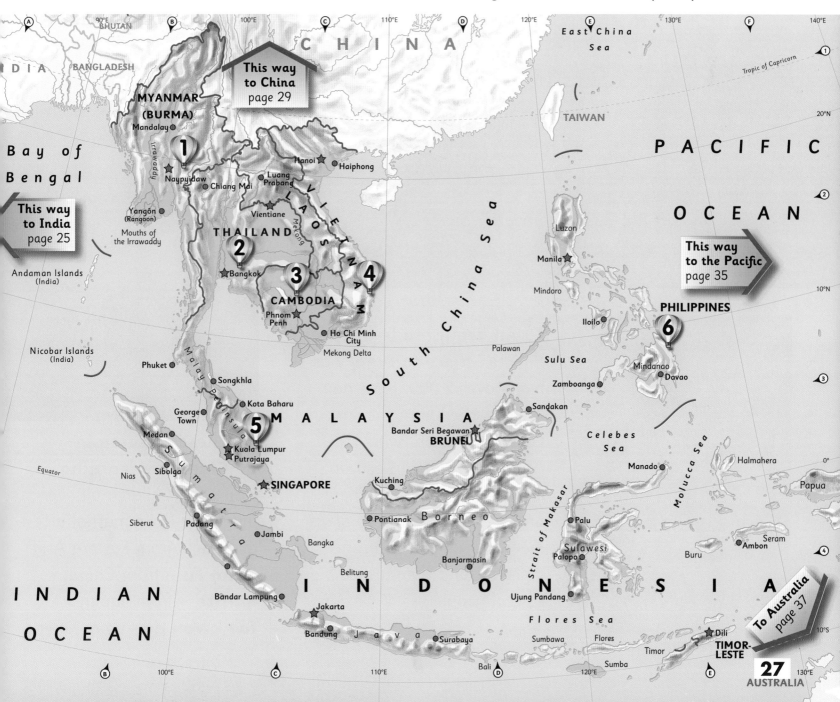

This way to China
page 29

This way to India
page 25

This way to the Pacific
page 35

To Australia
page 37

CHINA

BHUTAN
BANGLADESH
DIA
MYANMAR (BURMA)
Mandalay
Naypyidaw
Chiang Mai
Yangôn (Rangoon)
Mouths of the Irrawaddy
Bay of Bengal
Andaman Islands (India)
Nicobar Islands (India)
THAILAND
Bangkok
Luang Prabang
Vientiane
LAOS
Hanoi
Haiphong
VIETNAM
CAMBODIA
Phnom Penh
Ho Chi Minh City
Mekong Delta
Phuket
Songkhla
Kota Baharu
George Town
Medan
Kuala Lumpur
Putrajaya
MALAYSIA
SINGAPORE
Malay Peninsula
Sumatra
Nias
Sibolga
Padang
Siberut
Jambi
Bangka
Bandar Lampung
Belitung
Jakarta
Bandung
Java
Surabaya
INDIAN OCEAN
Equator
East China Sea
TAIWAN
Tropic of Capricorn
PACIFIC OCEAN
Luzon
Manila
Mindoro
PHILIPPINES
Iloilo
Mindanao
Davao
Palawan
Sulu Sea
Zamboanga
Sandakan
Bandar Seri Begawan
BRUNEI
South China Sea
Kuching
Borneo
Pontianak
Banjarmasin
Ujung Pandang
Celebes Sea
Manado
Palu
Sulawesi
Palopo
Buru
Molucca Sea
Halmahera
Papua
Seram
Ambon
Strait of Makasar
INDONESIA
Flores Sea
Sumbawa
Flores
Sumba
Bali
Timor
Dili
TIMOR-LESTE

Discover...
China and its Neighbours

1 The Bactrian camel (Asian camel) has **two humps** and can live in dry places that are hot or cold. A few wild camels still live in **Mongolia**.

2 **An army made of clay!** The Terracotta Army was made over 2,000 years ago. It was buried with the Emperor of Quin, who believed he would need an army in the after-life. There are over **8,000 figures** of men and horses! Each one is different, and they are as big as real people!

3 These children in China are learning **Kung Fu.** Children all over the world learn martial arts that came from Eastern Asia. **Kung Fu** – from China; **Karate** – from Japan; **Tae kwon do** – from Korea.

4 **China has many big cities** with big buildings and factories where lots of people live and work. Lots of things are made in China and sold all over the world.

6 **Japan has beautiful old palaces**, and flowering cherry trees in spring.

5 **Korea is split into 2 countries:** North Korea and South Korea.

North Korea flag

South Korea flag

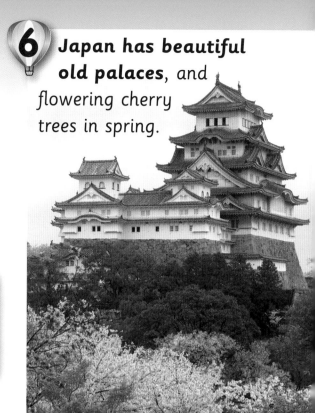

Scale 1:25,000,000 1 cm on the map = 250 km on the ground

| 0 | 250 km | 500 km | 1,000 km | 1,500 km | 2,000 km | 2,500 km | 3,000 km |

0 1 2 3 cm 4 5 6 7 8 9 cm 10 11 12

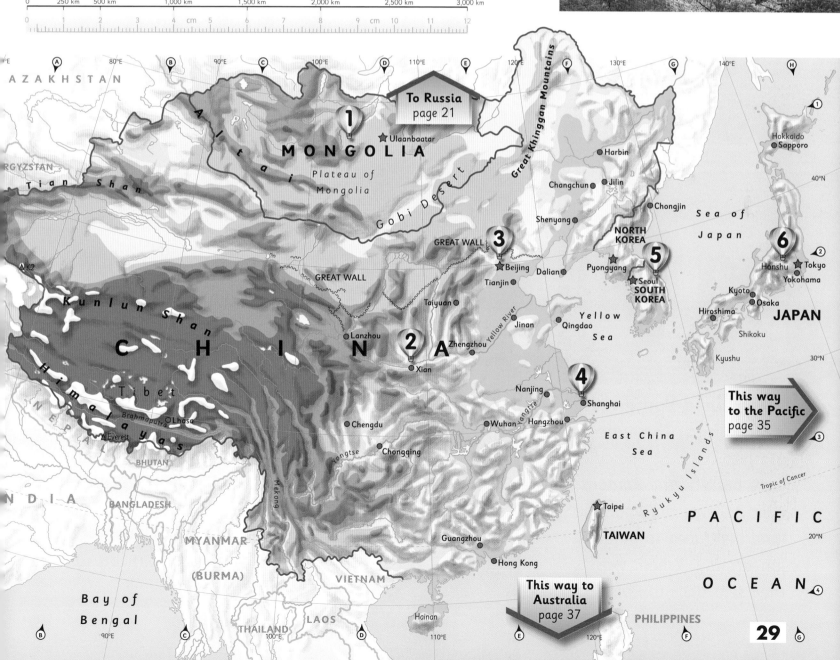

AZAKHSTAN

To Russia
page 21

1

MONGOLIA

☆ Ulaanbaatar

Plateau of Mongolia

Altai

Gobi Desert

Great Khinggan Mountains

● Harbin

GRYZSTAN

Tian Shan

Changchun ● ● Jilin

● Chongjin

Sea of Japan

40°N

Hokkaido
● Sapporo

1

Shenyang ●

GREAT WALL **3**

☆ Beijing ● Dalian

Pyongyang ●

NORTH KOREA

5

☆ Seoul
SOUTH KOREA

Honshu ☆ Tokyo
● Yokohama

6

2

K2 ▲

Kunlun Shan

GREAT WALL

Tianjin ●

Taiyuan ●

Jinan ●

Yellow River

Qingdao ●

Yellow Sea

Kyoto ●
Osaka ●

Hiroshima ●

JAPAN

Shikoku

C   H   I   N   **2**   A

Zhengzhou ●

Lanzhou ●

☆ Xian

Kyushu

30°N

Himalayas

Tibet

Brahmaputra
● Lhasa

NEPAL

▲ Everest

Chengdu ●

Chongqing ●

Yangtse

Nanjing ●

4

● Shanghai

Wuhan ● Hangzhou ●

East China Sea

This way to the Pacific
page 35

3

BHUTAN

Mekong

Ryukyu Islands

Tropic of Cancer

NDIA

BANGLADESH

MYANMAR

(BURMA)

VIETNAM

Guangzhou ●

● Hong Kong

☆ Taipei

TAIWAN

PACIFIC

20°N

Bay of Bengal

LAOS

THAILAND

Hainan ●

This way to Australia
page 37

PHILIPPINES

OCEAN

29

Discover...
North and West Africa

1 Egypt is an incredible country. The pyramids are here, and there are lots of big temples too. **Can you ...** find the **River Nile** on the map?

An oasis in the desert. Deserts are so dry that hardly any people, animals or plants can live there. But where there is **water** there is life.

2 **A ruined Roman city in Libya.** There are lots of ruins like this. The cities were built by the Romans over 2,000 years ago. The land here used to be good for farming. Wheat was then sent back to Rome.

3

What makes a camel so good at living in deserts? Their **thick fur** keeps camels cool in the day and warm at night. Their **wide feet** stop them sinking into loose sand and stones. Their **nostrils** shut so sand cannot blow in. And they can last a long time with **no water!**

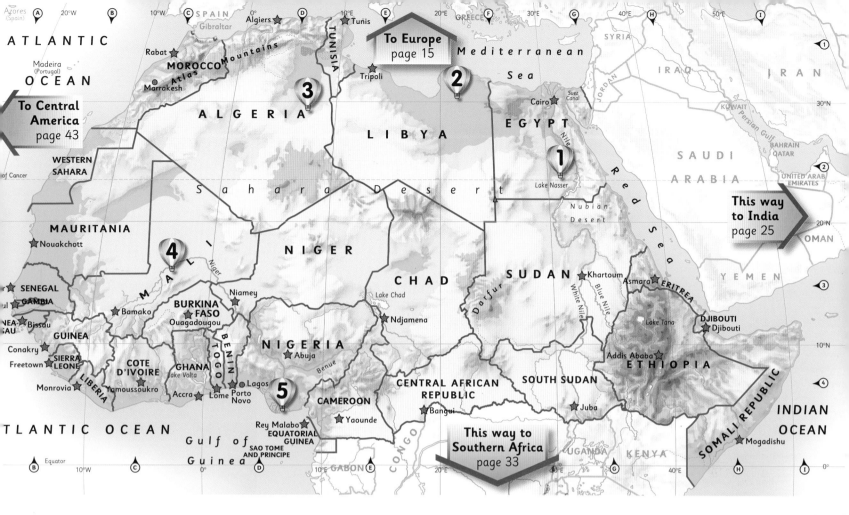

Scale 1:34,500,000 1 cm on the map = 345 km on the ground

0   345 km   1,000 km   2,000 km   3,000 km

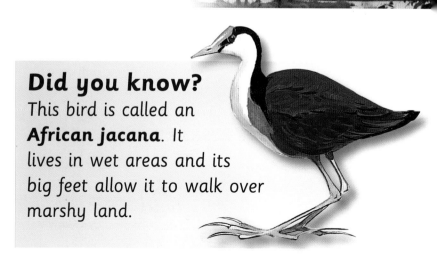

5 **Oil and gas in Nigeria.** Oil and gas have made a few Nigerians rich. But many people are still very poor and **pollution** is a big problem. Nigeria has more people than any country in Europe.

4 **A village in Mali.** These women are preparing a meal. Here there is a rainy season and a dry season. In June it rains and crops grow, but December is very hot and dry.

Did you know?
This bird is called an **African jacana**. It lives in wet areas and its big feet allow it to walk over marshy land.

To Europe page 15

To Central America page 43

This way to India page 25

This way to Southern Africa page 33

Discover...
Central and Southern Africa

1 **A baobab tree has such a fat trunk!** The long hot dry season is no problem for a baobab as it stores water in its amazing trunk! It is sometimes called an 'upside-down' tree because the fat stumpy branches look more like roots!

2 **Coffee grows best where daytime is very hot and the nights are cold.** High land in Uganda is just right for growing good coffee beans!

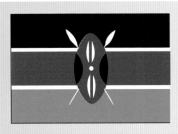

The flag of Kenya shows an African shield and 2 spears.
Black is for the African people.
Red is for the red blood of all people.
Green is for Kenya's rich agriculture.

3 **These stamps from Burundi** show a lion, a water buffalo, 2 hippos and a giraffe. Can you think of any other amazing animals in Africa?

Did you know?

There are 2 big long lakes in Africa – can you find them on the map?*
Long ago the land split apart, and this '**rift valley**' became deeper and wider.

4 **Elephants in the Namib Desert.**
Elephants are usually found on the grasslands but these live in the desert. Lions live here too!

5 **Johannesburg is a big city in South Africa.** Some hills are man-made: they are the waste rock from gold mines! The gold makes some people rich, but many people in Africa have very little money.

6 **SURPRISE!**
There are penguins on the south coast of South Africa – even though they are thousands of miles from Antarctica!

90c

Suid-Afrika
South Africa

DENIS MURPHY   SPHENISCUS DEMERSUS

A 10°E CAMEROON B   30°E SOUTH SUDAN D 40°E ETHIOPIA E 50°E F

To the rest
of Africa
page 31

EQUATORIAL
GUINEA
Libreville
GABON

CONGO
Congo
Basin

DEMOCRATIC REPUBLIC
OF
THE CONGO

Brazzaville
Kinshasa

CABINDA

Luanda

ANGOLA

2 UGANDA KENYA
Kampala Lake Nairobi Mount
Victoria Kenya
Kigali
3 RWANDA
Gitega Mount
BURUNDI Kilimanjaro Mombasa

TANZANIA
Lake Dodoma Zanzibar
Tanganyika

INDIAN
OCEAN

Equator 0°

Seychelles

This way
to Australia
page 37

To South
America
page 45

ZAMBIA
Lusaka Zambezi

MALAWI
Lake
Malawi
Lilongwe

MOZAMBIQUE

COMOROS
Moroni Mayotte
(France)

MADAGASCAR
Antananarivo

Mozambique Channel

Victoria Falls Harare
ZIMBABWE

4
NAMIBIA
Windhoek
Namib Desert

BOTSWANA
Kalahari
Desert
Gaborone

5
Pretoria
Johannesburg Mbabane
ESWATINI
Maputo

Limpopo

Reunion
(France)

Tropic of Capricorn

1

ATLANTIC OCEAN

SOUTH
AFRICA

LESOTHO
Maseru

This way to
Antarctica
page 47

INDIAN
OCEAN

6
Cape Town
Cape of
Good Hope

Scale 1:34,500,000   1 cm on the map = 345 km on the ground

345 km   1,000 km   2,000 km   3,000 km

Discover...
The Pacific

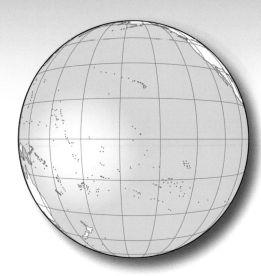

1 **The Mariana Trench is the deepest part of the ocean anywhere in the world.** Strange-looking creatures live in the deep ocean where daylight can never reach – like this one!

The Pacific is the biggest ocean in the world by far. It covers a third of the globe!

3 **A Southern Cassowary** – this large bird lives in the forests of New Guinea. But it cannot fly!

2 **High islands are volcanoes.** Volcanic soil is good for growing crops. But farmers must beware when a volcano is active, as it may erupt and send out lava.

Can you find these names on the maps?
Micronesia means 'little islands'.
Melanesia means 'black islands' – the sand is black from the volcanic rock.
Polynesia means 'lots of islands'.

4 **Low islands are coral islands.** The sand is white! People can live on these islands but flooding from the sea is a big worry. A **coral atoll** has calm sea in the centre, but round the edges of the atoll the sea is sometimes rough.

5 Hawaii is the 50th state of the USA.

Here in the Pacific Ocean the sea is deep and warm. Many visitors come to Hawaii to enjoy the surfing.

6 Pacific islanders at work.

This canoe has been **dug out** from **ONE** forest tree by these Pacific islanders. Thousands of years ago people sailed in search of land in boats like these, using the stars to find their way.

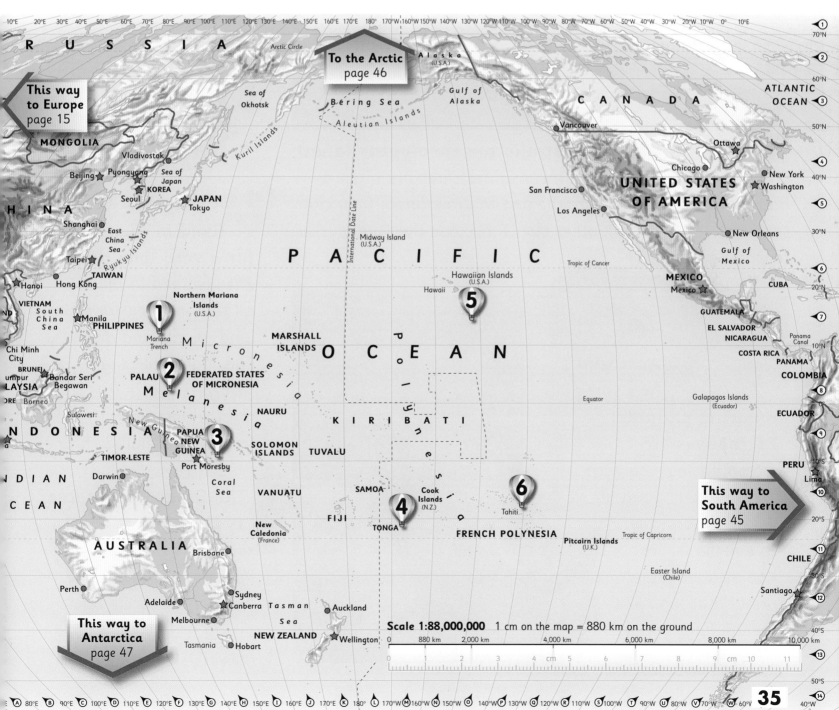

To the Arctic
page 46

This way to Europe page 15

This way to South America page 45

This way to Antarctica page 47

RUSSIA

Arctic Circle

Alaska (U.S.A.)

Sea of Okhotsk

Bering Sea

Gulf of Alaska

CANADA

ATLANTIC OCEAN

Vancouver

Ottawa

MONGOLIA

Vladivostok

Kuril Islands

Aleutian Islands

Chicago

New York

Beijing

Pyongyang

Sea of Japan

KOREA

San Francisco

Washington

UNITED STATES OF AMERICA

Seoul

JAPAN

Tokyo

Shanghai

East China Sea

Los Angeles

CHINA

Ryukyu Islands

New Orleans

Gulf of Mexico

Taipei

TAIWAN

Midway Island (U.S.A.)

P A C I F I C

Tropic of Cancer

Hanoi

Hong Kong

Hawaiian Islands (U.S.A.)

Hawaii

MEXICO

Mexico

CUBA

VIETNAM

South China Sea

Manila

PHILIPPINES

Northern Mariana Islands (U.S.A.)

MARSHALL ISLANDS

GUATEMALA

EL SALVADOR

NICARAGUA

Panama Canal

Chi Minh City

Mariana Trench

Micronesia

O C E A N

COSTA RICA

PANAMA

BRUNEI

umpur

Bandar Seri Begawan

PALAU

FEDERATED STATES OF MICRONESIA

Melanesia

COLOMBIA

LAYSIA

Borneo

NAURU

Equator

Galapagos Islands (Ecuador)

ECUADOR

Sulawesi

New Guinea

PAPUA NEW GUINEA

KIRIBATI

INDONESIA

Timor-Leste

Polynesia

SOLOMON ISLANDS

TUVALU

Port Moresby

PERU

Lima

Darwin

Coral Sea

SAMOA

Cook Islands (N.Z.)

NDIAN

VANUATU

Tahiti

CEAN

FIJI

TONGA

FRENCH POLYNESIA

Pitcairn Islands (U.K.)

Tropic of Capricorn

New Caledonia (France)

CHILE

AUSTRALIA

Brisbane

Easter Island (Chile)

Perth

Sydney

Adelaide

Canberra

Tasman Sea

Auckland

Santiago

Melbourne

NEW ZEALAND

Wellington

Tasmania

Hobart

Scale 1:88,000,000   1 cm on the map = 880 km on the ground

0   880 km   2,000 km   4,000 km   6,000 km   8,000 km   10,000 km

0   1   2   3   4   cm   5   6   7   8   cm   10   11

A 80°E   B 90°E   C 100°E   D 110°E   E 120°E   F 130°E   G 140°E   H 150°E   I 160°E   J 170°E   K 180°   L 170°W   M 160°W   N 150°W   O 140°W   P 130°W   Q 120°W   R 110°W   S 100°W   T 90°W   U 80°W   V 70°W   W 60°W

Discover...
Australia and New Zealand

1 Lots of trees in Australia are eucalyptus (gum) trees. The hot dry climate means forest fires are often a problem, but gum trees are the first to grow back. They can take over the land from other plants, because they are quicker to grow again.

2 Aborigines have lived in Australia for a very long time. They learned to make all they needed from the land, plants and animals. This man is playing a 'didgeridoo' – it is a musical instrument made from a long hollow branch.

Australia has some amazing animals. Platypuses are mammals, but lay eggs. The koala is good at climbing gum trees to eat the leaves. Koalas have finger prints that look like human finger prints!

3 The Great Barrier Reef is the biggest coral reef in the world. Visitors love to see the wonderful sea life by scuba-diving or looking through a glass-bottomed boat.

4 **Melbourne is the main city of the state of Victoria.** Australia has 7 states – can you find them on the map? All the biggest cities of Australia are near the sea.

Australia

New Zealand

SURPRISE! There's a flag from page 13 on these flags! The stars show the 'Southern Cross'. Can you see the differences?*

5 **Kiwis live in New Zealand.** These birds do not fly but come out at night and look for grubs to eat.

Can you find fruit from New Zealand? Look in shops for the labels.

Zespri GREEN 4030 NEW ZEALAND

NEW ZEALAND BRAEBURN #4101

ROYAL GALA 4173 PickMee! New Zealand

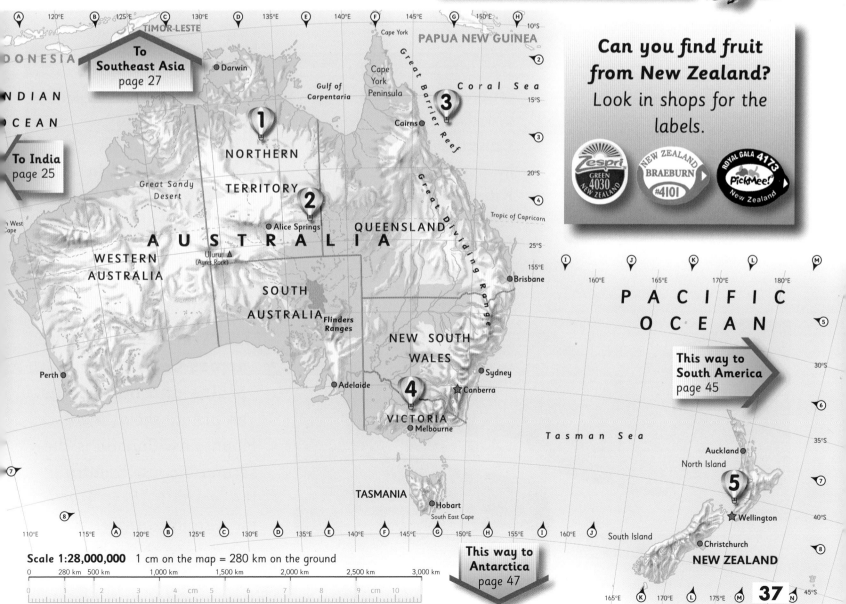

To Southeast Asia page 27

To India page 25

TIMOR-LESTE
INDONESIA
INDIAN OCEAN
Darwin
Gulf of Carpentaria
Cape York
PAPUA NEW GUINEA
Cape York Peninsula
Coral Sea
Cairns
Great Barrier Reef
Great Dividing Range
1 NORTHERN
Great Sandy Desert
TERRITORY
2
Alice Springs
QUEENSLAND
A U S T R A L I A
Uluru (Ayres Rock)
WESTERN AUSTRALIA
North West Cape
SOUTH AUSTRALIA
Flinders Ranges
Tropic of Capricorn
Brisbane
PACIFIC OCEAN
NEW SOUTH WALES
Perth
Adelaide
Sydney
Canberra
4
VICTORIA
Melbourne
This way to South America page 45
Tasman Sea
Auckland
North Island
TASMANIA
Hobart
South East Cape
South Island
5
Wellington
NEW ZEALAND
Christchurch

This way to Antarctica page 47

Scale 1:28,000,000 1 cm on the map = 280 km on the ground
0 280 km 500 km 1,000 km 1,500 km 2,000 km 2,500 km 3,000 km
0 1 2 3 4 cm 5 6 7 8 9 cm 10

Discover...
Canada and Alaska

1 **Alaska has amazing wildlife, like this Alaskan grizzly bear.** Alaska is part of the USA: the USA bought it from Russia in 1867. It is near Russia and partly in the Arctic. In winter it is very cold and days are short.

Do you know any Native American words?
Canada means 'village' in Mohawk.
Kayak is a boat like a canoe.
Wigwam and **Teepee**: these are types of tent.

2 **There is oil in Alaska.** This is an oil terminal on the Alaskan coast. Can you see 2 big tankers (ships)?

3 **This train travels right across Canada, over plains and mountains.** This picture shows the Rocky Mountains. Canada is the second biggest country in the world. It takes 4 days for a train to travel from one side to the other!

RUSSIA

ARCTIC OCEAN

GREENLAND
(Denmark)

ICELAND

ATLANTIC OCEAN

Bering Sea

Bering Strait

Beaufort Sea

Queen Elizabeth Islands

McClure Strait

Ellesmere Island

Baffin Bay

Denmark Strait

To the
North Pole
page 46

Yukon

Arctic Circle

Alaska
(USA)

Denali
(Mount McKinley)

Alaska Range

Alaska Peninsula

Anchorage

Gulf of Alaska

YUKON

Whitehorse

Skagway

This way
to Asia
page 29

PACIFIC OCEAN

Victoria Island

NORTHWEST TERRITORIES

Yellowknife

NUNAVUT

Hudson Bay

Baffin Island

Davis Strait

Hudson Strait

Labrador Sea

This way
to Europe
page 15

NEWFOUNDLAND AND LABRADOR

Labrador

Labrador City

Look at the map. Can you see the Rocky Mountains stretching down the western side of Canada and into the USA?

BRITISH COLUMBIA

Rocky Mountains

Fraser

ALBERTA

C A N A D A

SASKATCHEWAN

MANITOBA

Lake Winnipeg

ONTARIO

Q U E B E C

St Lawrence

St John's
Newfoundland

Gulf of St Lawrence

PRINCE EDWARD ISLAND

Vancouver Island

Vancouver

Victoria

Calgary

Regina

Winnipeg

Lake Superior

Quebec

Montreal

Ottawa

NEW BRUNSWICK

Fredericton

NOVA SCOTIA

Halifax

Cape Sable

Lake Michigan

Lake Huron

Toronto

Lake Ontario

Niagara Falls

Lake Erie

ATLANTIC OCEAN

UNITED STATES OF AMERICA

Scale 1:30,000,000   1 cm on the map = 300 km on the ground

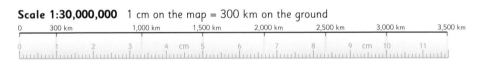

0   300 km   1,000 km   1,500 km   2,000 km   2,500 km   3,000 km   3,500 km

0   1   2   3   4 cm   5   6   7   8   9 cm   10   11

The Canadian flag has a red maple leaf on it. In autumn the maple leaves turn red. Some people say the hills turn red like fire.

The Niagara Falls are shared by Canada and the USA. They are between Lake Erie and Lake Ontario.

5 Newfoundland was named when Europeans 'found' it. This fishing village is **MUCH** closer to Europe than to western Canada!

Discover...
The USA

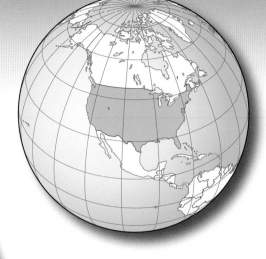

1 The Statue of Liberty was a gift from France over 100 years ago. It stands on an island in New York's harbour, and welcomes people who arrive by sea.

The bald eagle – America's national bird. This eagle is not really bald! The feathers on its head are pure white. It feeds on fish, mainly salmon.

3 Monument Valley. These amazing sandstone formations are in the Arizona desert. They are **huge**! Can you see a car at the bottom of the picture?

2 Harvesting wheat. Large machines called combine harvesters, like the red one in this picture, are used to harvest the grain.

Can you . . . find a long river with a long name on the map?* Here's a clue: •ISS•SSI••I

(Hint!)

4 The oldest living thing on Earth?

Bristlecone pine trees live for a very long time. Some of them are about 5,000 years old.

5 A tram station in downtown San Diego.

Trams are a great way to travel in cities: they travel fast on rails and they are clean and quiet.

Did you know?

The names of states tell us about the origins of the peoples of America:

Vermont – means 'green mountain' (French).

Nevada – means 'snowy' (Spanish).

Iowa – means 'beautiful land' (American Indian).

Scale 1:21,500,000   1 cm on the map = 215 km on the ground

0   215 km   500 km   1,000 km   1,500 km   2,000 km   2,500 km

0   1   2   3   4   cm   5   6   7   8   9   cm   10   11

To Canada and Alaska page 39

This way to Europe page 15

To the Pacific page 35

To Central America page 43

MASS = Massachusetts
CONN = Connecticut

UNITED STATES OF AMERICA

Discover...
Central America

1 Mexico is a big country. Mexico City is one of the biggest and busiest cities in the world. There are big deserts, mountains and volcanoes in Mexico.

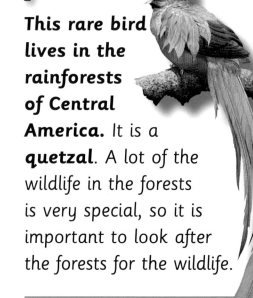

2 This rare bird lives in the rainforests of Central America. It is a **quetzal**. A lot of the wildlife in the forests is very special, so it is important to look after the forests for the wildlife.

NORTH AMERICA
Atlantic Ocean
Panama Canal
Pacific Ocean
SOUTH AMERICA

4 The flag of Jamaica:
Green – for farming
Gold – for sunshine
Black – for hardship

3 The Panama Canal is amazing – and useful too! Big ships can go from the **Pacific Ocean** to the **Atlantic Ocean**. How do you think ships could get from the Pacific to the Atlantic Ocean before this canal was dug?* Do you think it took a long time? The globe will help you!

6 **A carnival procession on Curaçao.** These women are enjoying a colourful street carnival. **SURPRISE!** Curaçao is a **Dutch** island.

5 **So many islands!** Tourists can travel on a ship and visit one island every day in the Caribbean. But beware of **hurricanes**!

Maize first came from Central America. Now it is grown all over the world. As well as corn-on-the-cob and sweetcorn, it is used for cornflakes and popcorn, and its flour is used in tortillas.

Bananas grow fast. This stamp shows bananas growing. Look hard at the stamp .... **Can you see** the green bananas growing – upwards?

7 ST. VINCENT 50c

BANANA CULTIVATION
GORDON DRUMMOND   1981   FORMAT

Scale 1:26,500,000   1cm on the map = 265 km on the ground

0   265km   1,000km   1,500km   2,000km   2,500km   3,000km   3,500km

0   1   2   3   4   cm   5   6   7   8   9   10   11   12   13cm

A   110°W   B   100°W   C   90°W   D   80°W   E

UNITED STATES OF AMERICA

Gulf of California

Sierra Madre

Rio Grande

This way to North America
page 39

30°N

Gulf of Mexico

This way to the Pacific
page 35

MEXICO **1**

110°W

Mexico City ☆

Acapulco ●

PACIFIC OCEAN

● Cancun

Yucatan

Cayman Islands

Havana ☆

CUBA

JAMAICA   Kingston ☆

4

HAITI
Port au Prince ☆

Belmopan ☆
BELIZE

Guatemala City ☆
GUATEMALA
San Salvador
EL SALVADOR   Tegucigalpa ☆

Managua ☆

HONDURAS

NICARAGUA

2

San Jose ☆
COSTA RICA

Panama ☆
PANAMA

3

This way to South America
page 45

10°N

90°W

D   80°W

2   70°W   F

BAHAMAS   A T L A N T I C   To Africa
page 31

☆ Nassau

5

Tropic of Cancer

O C E A N   60°W

Turks and Caicos Islands

20°N

DOMINICAN REPUBLIC

Santo Domingo ☆   San Juan   Virgin Islands (USA and UK)

Puerto Rico (USA)

ST KITTS-NEVIS

ANTIGUA AND BARBUDA

Guadeloupe (France)   3

C a r i b b e a n   S e a

DOMINICA

Martinique (France)

Aruba (Neths)   Curaçao (Neths)

6

ST LUCIA
ST VINCENT   **7**   BARBADOS

GRENADA

Port of Spain ☆
TRINIDAD 10°N
AND TOBAGO

VENEZUELA

COLOMBIA

GUYANA

E   70°W   F   G

On the map there is an island with **2** countries on it. In the west they speak **French**, but in the east they speak **Spanish**. What are the countries called?*

Discover...
South America

1 **A giant tortoise on the Galapagos Islands.** These volcanic islands are very far from other land. As a result, many special animals and plants only live here. **Can you** guess the age of the oldest giant tortoise?*

3 **Lake Titicaca is high up in the Andes.** These boats are made from reeds (surprise!), and they do float. It is so high up here that visitors get out of breath. **Can you** see which 2 countries share the lake?*

2 **The Amazon jungle is hot and wet.** The river is called the Amazon too! The trees are very big. There are so many different animals and plants here that no-one has ever seen them all. But some of the jungle is being chopped down.

4 **Buenos Aires.** This is the capital city of a big country – can you find it on the map?* 'Buenos Aires' means 'good air' in Spanish.

5 **The Atacama Desert in Chile.** This is the driest place in the world. The desert is very hot and dry. But the high Andes mountains are cold – with snow!

Which is the biggest cat in South America? It is the **jaguar**! Most jaguars live in the lowland rainforests near the Amazon River.

6 This is a '**monkey puzzle tree**'. It grows in the south of Chile – its real name is a '**Chilean pine**'.
Is it chilly in Chile?
Sometimes! It is cold in the high mountains and in the south of Chile. But it is hot in the desert and in the summer (December) in central Chile.

Can you find how many countries touch Brazil?*

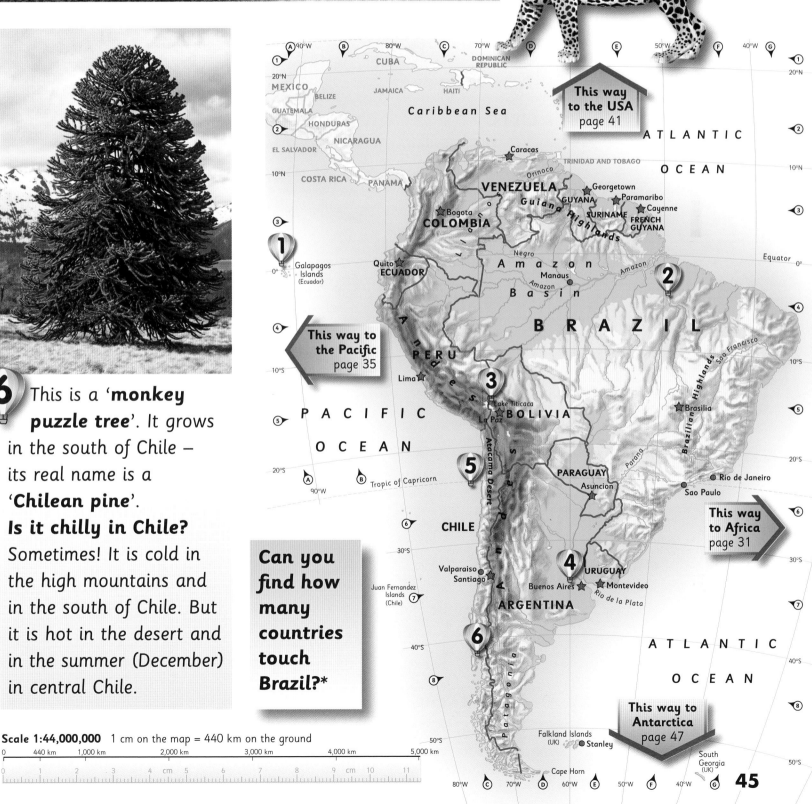

This way to the USA
page 41

This way to the Pacific
page 35

This way to Africa
page 31

This way to Antarctica
page 47

CUBA
DOMINICAN REPUBLIC
MEXICO
BELIZE
JAMAICA
HAITI
GUATEMALA
HONDURAS
EL SALVADOR
NICARAGUA
COSTA RICA
PANAMA
Caribbean Sea
ATLANTIC OCEAN
Caracas
TRINIDAD AND TOBAGO
Orinoco
VENEZUELA
Georgetown
Guiana GUYANA
Paramaribo
Cayenne
Bogota
SURINAME
FRENCH GUYANA
COLOMBIA
Highlands
Negro
Amazon
Equator
Galapagos Islands (Ecuador)
Quito
ECUADOR
Amazon
Manaus
Amazon
Basin
BRAZIL
PERU
Andes
São Francisco
Lima
Brazilian Highlands
Lake Titicaca
Brasilia
BOLIVIA
La Paz
PACIFIC OCEAN
Atacama Desert
Parana
PARAGUAY
Asuncion
Rio de Janeiro
Pampas
Tropic of Capricorn
Sao Paulo
CHILE
Valparaiso
Santiago
URUGUAY
Buenos Aires
Montevideo
Rio de la Plata
Juan Fernandez Islands (Chile)
ARGENTINA
ATLANTIC OCEAN
Patagonia
Falkland Islands (UK)
Stanley
South Georgia (UK)
Cape Horn

Scale 1:44,000,000 1 cm on the map = 440 km on the ground

0   440 km   1,000 km   2,000 km   3,000 km   4,000 km   5,000 km

0   1   2   3   4   cm   5   6   7   8   9   cm   10   11

Discover...
The Arctic

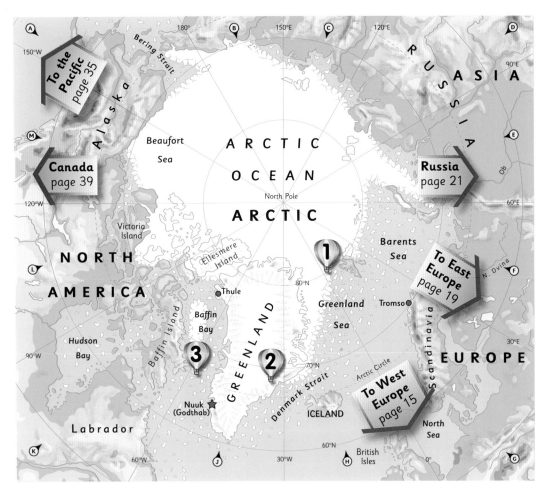

To the Pacific page 35

Canada page 39

Russia page 21

To East Europe page 19

To West Europe page 15

Bering Strait

Alaska

Beaufort Sea

ARCTIC

OCEAN

North Pole

ARCTIC

Victoria Island

Ellesmere Island

NORTH

AMERICA

Thule

Baffin Island

Baffin Bay

GREENLAND

Greenland Sea

Denmark Strait

ICELAND

Arctic Circle

Scandinavia

EUROPE

Barents Sea

Tromso

N. Dvina

Ob

RUSSIA

ASIA

Hudson Bay

Nuuk (Godthab)

Labrador

North Sea

British Isles

Scale 1:50,000,000 1 cm on the map = 500 km on the ground

0   500 km   1,000 km   2,000 km   4,000 km   6,000 km   8,000 km   10,000 km

0   1   2   3   4   cm   5   6   7   8   9   cm   10   11   12

2 Greenland is mostly white with ice, not green! This owl is white so it is hard to see when there is snow.

AMAZING! In the **ARCTIC**, there are 24 hours of **daylight** in **June** and 24 hours of **darkness** in **December**.

1 Polar bears live in the Arctic. They are the biggest of all the bears. They hunt for fish and seals.

3 People live in the Arctic. This Inuit hunter and his dogsled team are travelling on the frozen polar sea of Baffin Bay.

*Find answers on page 48

Discover... Antarctica

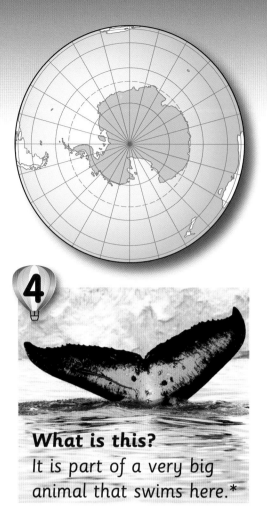

1 **Penguins live in the Antarctic**. They can't fly but they are brilliant swimmers.

AMAZING! In the **ANTARCTIC**, there are 24 hours of **darkness** in **June** and 24 hours of **daylight** in **December**.

2 **Can you name these flags?** They are some of the countries that have bases in Antarctica.*

3 **Some tourists come to see Antarctica by boat.** Beware of icebergs!

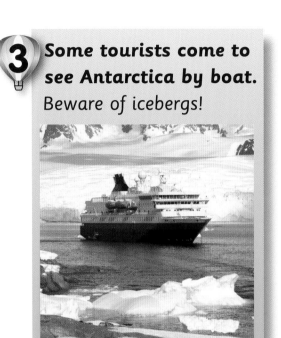

4 **What is this?** It is part of a very big animal that swims here.*

Scale 1:50,000,000 1 cm on the map = 500 km on the ground

0	500 km	1,000 km	2,000 km	4,000 km	6,000 km	8,000 km	10,000 km

0   1   2   3   4 cm 5   6   7   8   9 cm 10   11   12

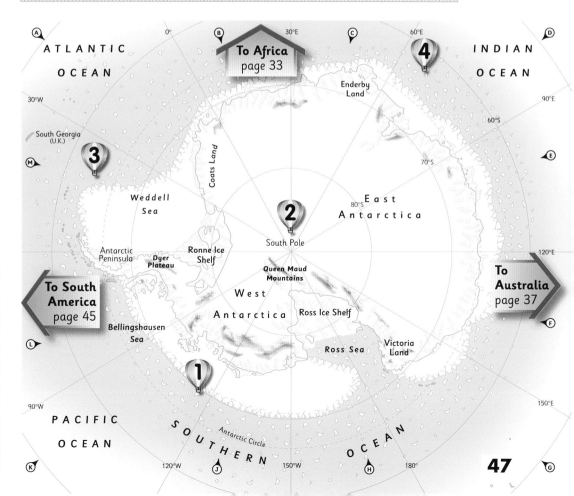

ATLANTIC OCEAN

To Africa page 33

INDIAN OCEAN

Enderby Land

30°W

South Georgia (U.K.)

Coats Land

East Antarctica

Weddell Sea

South Pole

Antarctic Peninsula   Dyer Plateau   Ronne Ice Shelf

Queen Maud Mountains

To South America page 45

West Antarctica   Ross Ice Shelf

Bellingshausen Sea

To Australia page 37

Victoria Land

Ross Sea

90°W

PACIFIC OCEAN

SOUTHERN OCEAN

Antarctic Circle

120°W   150°W   180°

47

Index

Answers to Questions

Page 10 USA, Brazil and Nigeria.

Page 19 New countries are Estonia, Latvia, Lithuania, Belarus, Ukraine, Moldova, Czechia, Slovakia, Slovenia, Croatia, Bosnia, Serbia, Montenegro, Kosovo, North Macedonia.
2 big seas are Baltic and Black.

Page 21 The Caspian Sea is shared by Russia, Kazakhstan, Turkmenistan, Azerbaijan and Iran.

Page 22 The three continents are Africa, Asia and Europe.

Page 23 The biggest country is Saudi Arabia. The stamp shows 2 palm trees, 3 fruit trees, farmland, a village and a tower.

Page 33 Lake Tanganyika and Lake Malawi.

Page 37 Australia's flag has 6 stars. New Zealand's flag has 4 stars.

Page 40 Mississippi River.

Page 42 Ships had to go all the way around South America. See map on page 45.

Page 43 In Haiti the people speak French – in the Dominican Republic people speak Spanish.

Page 44 The oldest giant tortoise was 152 years old. Lake Titicaca is shared by Peru and Bolivia. Buenos Aires is the capital city of Argentina.

Page 45 10 countries touch Brazil.

Page 47 The flags are from New Zealand, Chile, Norway, Argentina, United Kingdom and France.
The picture is of the tail of a whale.

Photo Acknowledgements

Robin Aiello (Ocean Antics Consulting) 36 centre bottom; **Alamy** /Ashley Cooper 13 top left, /David Lomax/Robert Harding Picture Library Ltd 14 top left, /Zaichiki 18 bottom left, /Bert de Ruiter 18 bottom right, /Iain Masterton 20 top right, /Oleg Moiseyenko 20 bottom left, /Dinodia Images 25 top left, /FAN travelstock 30 centre left, /Friedrich Stark 31 centre right, /Images&Stories 32 top left, /Images of Africa Photobank 31 top right, /Chad Ehlers 34 bottom, /Sami Sarkis Lifestyles 35 top right, /Terry Fincher.Photo Int 38 top right, /blickwinkel 41 top left, /World Pictures 42 top left, /VI 43 top centre, /JUPITERIMAGES/Creatas 44 top left, /Amazon-Images 44 bottom left, /Chad Ehlers 44 bottom right; **City of Johannesburg** /Walter Knirr 33 top right; **Corbis** /Gabe Palmer/zefa 2 centre right, /Image Plan (RF) 6 montage top left, /Image100 (RF) 6 montage top right, /Robert Glusic (RF) 6 montage bottom left, /Kristi J. Black (RF) 6 montage bottom right, /Pawel Libera 12 top left, /Felix

Ordonez/Reuters 16 top left, /Kevin Burke 18 bottom centre, /Goodshoot 20 top left, /Reuters 23 top left, /Paul Almasy 24 top left, /Steven Vidler /Eurasia Press 25 top right, /Jacques Langevin 28 top left, /Keren Su 28 centre right, /Yann Arthus-Bertrand 30 top left, /Bruno Fert 31 bottom left, /Image100 (RF) top left, /George Steinmetz 34 centre left, /Paul A. Souders 36 top left, /Claire Leimbach/Robert Harding World Imagery 36 top right, /Erwin & Peggy Bauer/zefa 38 top left, /Danny Lehman 42 centre left, /DLILLC (RF) 46 bottom left, /Layne Kennedy 46 bottom right; **Dreamstime.com** /Gibbsterr 12 top right, /Railpix 12 bottom left, /Lastdays1 14 bottom left, /Kurt 14 bottom right, /Britvich 15 centre right, /Gnugent 17 centre left, /Dmitryp 20 bottom right, /Ronnachai Limpakdeesavasd 24 centre right, /Nalukai 35 top left, /Lesterlester 44 centre right, /Eg004713 45 top left, /Wildernessphotographs 45 centre right, /Bernardbreton 47 bottom left, /Cascoly 47 top centre; **Fotolia.com** /bobroy20 16 bottom right, /RadioUran 21 top left, /Alena Yakusheva 26 bottom left (and back cover), /Stephan Karg 30 bottom centre;

iStockphoto.com /Rolf Weschke 13 top right, /Daniel Breckwoldt 15 top left, /Branislav Bubanja 16 bottom left, /Ricardo De Mattos 17 top left, /Angelafoto 17 top right, /ewg3D 18 top left, /Ferenc Vágvölgyi 19 bottom left, /Andrey Kolganov 20 centre (and back cover), /Rob Broek 21 top right, /Steven Allan 22 top left, /Alena Yakusheva 22 bottom left, /David Ciemny 24 bottom left, /x-drew 24 bottom right, /Robert Churchill 26 top left, /Martyn Smith 26 bottom right, /Paolo Santoné 27 top right, /Alan Tobey 28 bottom left, /real444 29 top left, /Ralph Paprzycki 29 top right, /xavierarnau 37 top left, /YinYang 38 bottom, /Richard Gunion 39 bottom centre, /Allan Morrison 39 bottom right, /Tony Campbell 40 centre left, /holgs 41 top centre, /Steve Geer 43 top left, /Carol Gray 46 top right, /Mark Fitzsimmons 47 top right; **NASA/GSFC** Reto Stockli, Alan Nelson, Fritz Hasler 6 top; **NPA Satellite Mapping** 5 bottom, 8 top; **Caroline Ohara** 40 bottom right; **Oxford Scientific (OSF)** /Paulo de Oliveira 34 top left; **Shutterstock** /seewhatmitchsee 15 top, /rasoulali 22 bottom right, /achinthamb 40 top left.

48

Glossary

Have fun with this page: match the pictures on this page with pictures in the main atlas.

Border – the line where 2 countries meet. Borders are shown as red lines on the maps.

Canal – a man-made river, dug by people for boats to travel on. Spot one on page 42.

Capital city – the city where the government of the country meets. This city is on page 42.

Continent – the largest areas of land. There are 7 continents on Earth, shown on page 10.

Coral – tiny sea animals; when they die their shells become like rocks. Pages 34 and 36.

Country – an area of land that is ruled by its own government.

Crops – plants grown by people to use for food. See how many crops you can find in this atlas. Try pages 17, 18, 25, 26, 32, 40 and 43.

Desert – a big area of land where it is very, very dry. Find deserts on pages 30, 40 and 45.

Farming – using land to grow crops or keep animals, usually for food.

Globe – a map of the world that is printed on a sphere (ball shape). Find a globe on page 1 and page 7.

Irrigation – watering crops to keep the plants alive. You can find this stamp on page 23.

Lake – an area of water that is surrounded by land. Find this lake on page 20.

Mining – digging up things people want from under the ground. See page 33.

Mountains – land which is high, and usually steep and rocky too. See mountains on pages 13, 15, 24, 38 and 45.

Oasis – a place in a desert where there is water. See page 30.

Pollution – when people put things into the air, soil or water that make them dirty and not safe.

Transport – moving people or things. How many different sorts of transport can you find in this Atlas?

Tundra – land in the far north where it is so cold it is always frozen underneath. See page 21.

Volcano – a mountain with a hole in the top that sometimes sends out melted rock (lava), in a sudden explosion. See page 34.

Country flags from around the World

 Lesotho

 Liberia

 Libya

 Liechtenstein

Lithuania

Luxembourg

 Macedonia North

 Mauritania

 Mauritius

 Mexico

Micronesia

 Moldova

 Monaco

 Mongolia

 Netherlands

New Zealand

 Nicaragua

 Niger

 Nigeria

 Northern Marianas

 Norway

Poland

 Portugal

 Puerto Rico

Qatar

Romania

Russia

 Rwanda

 Singapore

 Slovakia

 Slovenia

 Solomon Islands

 Somalia

 South Africa

Spain

 Sweden

 Switzerland

 Syria

 Taiwan

 Tajikistan

Tanzania

 Thailand

 Tuvalu

 Uganda

 Ukraine

 United Arab Emirates

 United Kingdom

 United States of America

 Uruguay